MW01688909

HOW TO LIVE ABOVE FEAR AND ANXIETY

by

Bill Basansky

Harrison House
Tulsa, Oklahoma

Unless otherwise indicated, all Scripture quotations are taken from the *King James Version* of the Bible.

Scripture quotations marked AMP are taken from *The Amplified Bible, New Testament.* Copyright © 1954, 1958 by the Lockman Foundation, La Habra, California.

How To Live Above Fear and Anxiety
ISBN 0-89274-058-2
Copyright © 1977 by Bill Basansky
P. O. Box 7126
Fort Myers, Florida 33911

Published by Harrison House, Inc.
P.O. Box 35035
Tulsa, Oklahoma 74153

Printed in the United States of America.
All rights reserved under International Copyright Law. Contents and/or cover may not be reproduced in whole or in part in any form without the express written consent of the Publisher.

Contents

Preface

> **Herein is our love made perfect, that we may have boldness in the day of judgment: because as he is, so are we in this world.**
>
> **There is no fear in love; but *perfect love casteth out fear:* because fear hath torment. He that feareth is not made perfect in love.**
>
> **We love him, because he first loved us.**
>
> **If a man say, I love God, and hateth his brother, he is a liar: for he that loveth not his brother whom he hath seen, how can he love God whom he hath not seen?**
>
> **And this commandment have we from him, That he who loveth God love his brother also.**
>
> **1 John 4:17-21**

In this scripture we clearly see that Christ is the complete answer to all problems: fears and anxiety that can't be dealt with by a formula, but the *Person, Jesus Christ.*

Fear is the symptom that stems from a deep root of disobedience by Adam in the Garden; but we must understand the difference between (wrong kind) sinful fear and the (right kind) danger fear that requires protection for your own life or the life of others.

1
Sinful Fear

Sinful fear or unreal fear appeared first in the Bible in Genesis 3:10 when Adam sinned and hid behind a bush. Sinful fears can be easily recognized for what they are when we look through the eyes of *Christ*:

1. Fear of God who is waiting for us to make a mistake so that He can punish us, make us sick, etc.

2. Fear of death, disease, germs, old age, fear of water, fear of failure, fear of airplanes, fear of what other people think of us, fear of authority.

The Bible says, **He that feareth is not made perfect in love** (1 John 4:18). **But whoso keepeth his word, in him verily is the love of God perfected**... (1 John 2:5).

Doctors say that 80 percent of people in hospitals today cannot be cured with medicine. They are being destroyed by *sinful fear, hatred, anger, unforgiveness, bitterness,* etc. All of these are from the same source because they have the same father, the devil.

In 1 John 4:18 the Bible says: **Perfect love casteth out fear.** In reading that scripture our logical mind would suggest to us that the opposite of fear is peace. Therefore, we might conclude, it should be peace that casts out all fear. But the Bible says *perfect love casts out fear.* Fear causes a person to hide and withdraw inwardly.

Love is open even if the enemy is there. Love stretches its arms openly and is ready to give. You might say, what if you get hurt? Love is not afraid of hurt; love removes hurt. Study the first Adam and you will see that his sin invited fear in, and he ran and hid from God. Study the second Adam — Jesus Christ who had no sin, but perfect love with the Father. He became angry at sin but never fearful. Even on the cross, with a deep sense of love and compassion, He said, "Father, forgive them for they know not what they are doing."

The difference between the *fear of death* and *apprehension of death:*

1. *Fear of death* is because we know that there is a judgment for our sins, and it's a reminder that we (unlike God) cannot control time or death.

2. *Apprehension of death* is wondering what it will be like. Why is it that some people are afraid of flying? Is it not because they fear placing themselves in another person's hands?

And it is also true that when we are challenged to place ourselves in God's hands, we often fail to trust even Him (let alone the pilot of an airplane!). We have difficulty trusting anyone with any power except ourselves. When I am in control, then I have no fear.

Why are we afraid of failure? We think of ourselves as a great somebody, and we don't want people to see our faults. Therefore, we would rather not make *any* decisions or do *anything* than to make a mistake and show people that we're not perfect. We would rather hide behind our mask or a bush (as Adam did) than to repent and admit our faults.

In the Garden of Eden we find God coming into the garden and discovering Adam and Even hiding away. He calls to them, and Adam says: "Lord we are hiding behind the bush, we are naked."

And God began to deal with them about their nakedness. God said, "Why are you hiding; what's the trouble?"

Adam says, "I was *afraid* and I hid myself." The first nervous breakdown began right back there in the Garden of Eden, and it began through fear as a result of *sin.*

> **And they heard the voice of the Lord God walking in the garden in the cool of the day: and Adam and his wife hid themselves from the presence of the Lord God amongst the trees of the garden.**

And the Lord God called unto Adam, and said unto him, Where art thou?

And he said, I heard thy voice in the garden, and I was afraid, because I was naked; and I hid myself.

Genesis 3:8-10

All sickness and disease of any kind has its roots in the first cause of sin, going back to Adam. Adam said, "I was afraid and I hid myself." That is what fear does. Sin and sickness, disease and death are the result of sin which makes us want to hide and shut ourselves away. The nature of fear is hate. Behind hate is murder, and murder is the nature of Satan. The Bible says he (the devil) was **a murderer from the beginning and the father of lies** (John 8:44).

2

Fear Hath Torment

In 1 John 4:18 the Bible says: **Fear hath torment.** I want you to think about that. *Fear hath torment.* Fear *opens* the *door* to suicide, murder, hate, etc. Fear is the opposite of love, and love, of course, is the very nature of God (1 John 4:7,8).

Fear causes us to hide from the presence of God, behind bushes, doors and garments of leaves like Adam and Eve. Adam said, "I am afraid, I am scared, because I have sinned against God. I know I am not right with you, the sense of your presence is gone; as a result, I am fearful; I am afraid, I have to hide." We discover that fear actually makes people *introverts* who hide and live their lives shut within themselves. It produces what we find in the Bible to be a "closed-door" experience.

In John 20:19 we read about the disciples of the Lord, and what they were doing. They were hiding behind closed doors; the doors were shut, and they didn't want to be discovered. They didn't want to come out. The Bible says **the wicked flee when no man pursueth** (Prov. 28:1). You may not be wicked, but you may have fear from the wicked one. Fear drives us into ourselves and we hide behind bushes, garments, and closed doors.

In Matthew 14:30 we read the story of Peter walking on the water. The Bible tells us that he was afraid, and then he began to sink. This is what fear does to you.

Many people don't know themselves and have forgotten what they are really like because of fear. Oh, friends, I want to tell you that fear is of the devil and it produces torment.

In 1 John 3:8 the Bible says Jesus came into the world to destroy the works of the devil. And if there is one thing that Jesus wants to do after He has forgiven your sins, it is to bring you out of yourself; from behind closed doors, bushes — out of your own shell.

The reason we are not doing more for God today is because fear is gripping the minds and hearts of God's people. This is not right. God is not pleased. Thank God, we have an answer, and the answer is found in Jesus Christ. In Matthew 14:30 we read that Peter began to sink because of fear. But as he called on Jesus Christ and looked to Him, Jesus came and saved him, and set him free (John 8:32,36).

Fear hides away in personality and can be clearly detected in a person's eyes. When you become free you will be as a butterfly. It will be the beginning of a new day and the starting of a new life for you.

3
Fear Destroys

In John 10:10 Jesus said,

> **The thief cometh not but for to steal, and to kill, and to destroy: I am come that they might have life, and that they might have it more abundantly.**

Satan comes to steal, kill, to put fear into the souls of people and to destroy. Satan's fear produces actual disease that is capable of destroying its victims.

As a young boy living in the Soviet Union, I was frightened by the noise of a small pig that was brought into a dark room in which I was sitting by the the babysitter. The experience was so dramatic that it caused me to have nightmares most of my adult life. However, when I became a Christian and recognized that this fear was not of God, I renounced it and in the name of Jesus Christ commanded the spirit of fear that tormented me with nighmares to depart out of my life. Because of my authority through the name and the shed blood of our Lord Jesus Christ, the spirit of fear departed my life, and I haven't had any nightmares since. Praise the Lord!

My wife, Bea, on one occasion as we traveled to Africa and Europe to minister the Word of God, became so exhausted physically that the devil began to bombard her with painful symptoms in her body, but expecially in her chest.

While I was out in the field ministering, the devil was working overtime on Bea. She resisted the devil with the Word, but the symptoms grew worse. Fear began to attack her mind to the point that she became weak in her physical and spiritual body.

Finally, when we came back from Africa, she called our doctor friend (who is a Spirit-filled Christian) for his advice.

Having spoken to her over the phone, he insisted that she come to his office for an examination. The x-rays showed that she had pneumonia in her lungs, and he prescribed medications and rest.

When Bea was assured of what the symptoms were, she also realized who caused it. At that very moment she took authority over the spirit of fear and infirmity, cast it out and commanded the symptoms of pneumonia to depart also. Sometimes the unknown can be a place for fear to attack, and it binds us from receiving our healing. As soon as she overcame the fear, her body began to recover immediately. In a few days she was completely well. It is true that she took the prescribed medication, but the quick and total recovery was due to the spiritual battle that was won in her mind. It came when she, with confidence, took the authority and rebuked the fearful and tormenting thoughts in the name of Jesus Christ.

There was never a disease that was not subject to the name of Jesus. But there are many men and women unable to find deliverance, not because their disease cannot be cured, but because they are harboring fear, anger, unforgiveness, etc. I want to tell you that sickness and infirmity can be caused by a germ, by a bullet or by an uncontrolled tongue, or by unruly children, rebellion, jealousy or a guilt complex. A deep rooted fear can bring about sickness, disease, and finally, death.

People often say, even some Christians: ''Don't drink a glass of water after me, don't come close to me, because I have a cold, flu or some other symptom of the devil.'' This suggests to the hearer that he should stay away from that individual. Then the spirit of fear attacks that person and suggests to him, by a lying symptom, that he too is getting sick. And when you agree with the devil and the symptom, you will get sick.

If it's true that a person can catch a sickness by any of these bad fruits (transmitted germs), then the opposite is just as true. When we conduct ourselves and live even as Christ commands us, and partake of good fruit (His unfailing promises), we will have health for the whole man.

According to the Word of God, all I have to do is lay my hands on you and impart some of the healthy fruit (gifts of healing) in Jesus' name, and the power of God begins to heal you (Mark 16:17,18). The moment I touch you by the laying on of hands, the Bible says it will stir up the gift of God within you (2 Tim. 1:6). After all, if people can infect or transmit harmful fruit (bacteria) into a person, then why can I not transmit or impart to people good, healthy fruit (life and health) in Christ's name.

I am not afraid of disease. I am not afraid of germs. It wouldn't trouble me to walk into an infectious hospital ward and pray for people, because greater is He that is within me, than he that is in the world.

4
The Posion of Fear

There are chemical changes that take place in the blood stream of people who are suffering with fear. Fear actually cripples and paralyzes people. It robs a man of his nobility and makes him a slave.

Have you ever heard people talk like this: ''You make me sick,'' or, ''He (she) makes me sick.'' Many, many people are sick and diseased in their bodies because they are unhappy with other people.

Some people have gone to the healing service and have expected the man of God to work some kind of a miracle that is going to bring healing to their bodies. But too often, the sickness is produced not by disease or organic structure, but by a blood stream that is constantly polluted from an untamed tongue filled with deadly poison (James 3:8), or resentment, bitterness and fear retained in the mind, which prevents God from granting them their desires. Doctors call this kind of condition *psychosomatic* and it's very real, *but the Bible calls it sin.*

Have you ever heard people say, ''You drive me up the wall; you drive me crazy! It blows my mind; It scared me to death; I was white as a ghost with fear; I was boiling with anger.'' What do these things tell us?

They tell us two things:

1. Every person thinks in pictures. Before they can say a word, they must recognize a picture in their mind's eye. After it's been recognized, then they say it with their mouth, and with their spoken words they give life or death.

> **Death and life are in the power of the tongue: and they that love it shall eat the fruit thereof.**
>
> **Proverbs 18:21**

Therefore, when you say, "You drive me crazy," you have agreed with the devil when he put that picture in your mind, and you said it with your mouth that you are crazy. But the Word of God says that God has not given you a crazy mind, but a sound mind. Therefore, do not agree with the devil; agree with God, for by your words *you* will be justified or condemned.

> **But I say unto you, That every idle word that men shall speak, they shall give account thereof in the day of judgment.**
>
> **For by thy words thou shalt be justified, and by thy words thou shalt be condemned.**
>
> **Matthew 12:36,37**

2. Doctors tell us that fear or emotional disturbances of any kind produce chemical changes in the blood stream. These chemical changes produce a variety of symptoms including disease in the body. So what do you want? Do you want to be healed of your symptoms or do you want to be rid of the cause?

We need to be right, not only with God but with our fellow man. In fact, we cannot be right with God if we are wrong with any human being on earth, especially with ourselves.

The questions that I want to ask of us all are these: How many people have we killed with our unkind words? How many people are responsible for killing *you* by their unkind words? How many people are you afraid of because of their unkind deeds?

I am telling you something, friend. You cannot afford to be afraid. No matter who you are, where you come from, or what your circumstances are, you cannot be afraid, because God commands us to serve Him without fear.

> **That he would grant unto us, that we being delivered out of the hand of our enemies might serve him without fear.**
>
> **Luke 1:74**

For God hath not given us the spirit of fear; but of power, and of love, and of a sound mind.

2 Timothy 1:7

If fear gets a hold on you, it will destroy you. It will produce chemical reactions and changes in your blood stream, and those chemical changes will produce the symptoms of sickness, disease, and other works of the devil.

I believe that we ought to love one another. This is what the Bible teaches: Children ought to obey and love their parents.

Children, obey your parents in the Lord: for this is right.

Honor thy father and mother; (which is the first commandment with promise;)

That it may be well with thee, and thou mayest live long on the earth.

Ephesians 6:1-3

Children, obey your parents in all things: for this is well pleasing unto the Lord.

Fathers, provoke not your children to anger, lest they be discouraged.

Colossians 3:20,21

And, ye fathers, provoke not your children to wrath: but bring them up in the nurture and admonition of the Lord.

Ephesians 6:4

If we don't obey the Bible, what is going to happen? There is going to be turmoil, confusion, conflict, arguments, and out of all this comes *fear, resentment* and *anxiety.* And out of these come a poisoned blood stream that brings sickness and death.

5

Fear Frustrates

While studying "safety courses" in college, I was amazed to discover the statistics and the percentage of accidents that are caused in our nation as a result of emotional upsets. This percentage applies to not only our domestic and traffic accidents, but to industry as well. The National Safety Council tells us that 85 percent of all automobile accidents happen within 10 miles of where an emotional upset has occurred. What am I saying? I am saying that accidents, too often, don't just *happen*. They are emotionally created. Because we struggle and strive emotionally, it brings about circumstances that are conducive to accidents. It is not by chance that these accidents occur.

Emotional upsets can come about when we neglect one another and fail to help or communicate with one another. Let's assume that you and I are sitting in the living room in conversation and fellowship. What a wonderful time we are having playing at being spiritual, or sharing a blessed experience, or preaching up a storm. We're not a bit concerned about the wife who is shut up there in the kitchen preparing the meals, washing the dishes, and looking after three small children that are screaming at the top of their lungs.

Well, she has put up a tremendous fight thus far. She's done about as much as she can. I mean she has been out there listening to you brag. . .it would be interesting to know all the things she has been saying under her breath about you and your friends! You are in there telling your friends and relations how grand it is to be a Christian, while she is out there having to do all the chores that need to be done to entertain your friends. Not once, but twice, week in and week out, month after month, year in and year out.

This time she can stand it no longer. So in the process of making the dessert and coffee, because she is upset and disturbed, she suddenly becomes clumsy. Somehow she manages to drop the pot and spill the coffee. As a result, the hot coffee has badly blistered her arms and legs. She cries out, and immediately the cry is heard, and everyone comes running from the living room and they start to make a fuss over this woman who is all blistered and burned. And what do they say? They say, "Let me help you with that, dear. It's not fair that you should be out here struggling. I should have been out here helping you." Now she starts to feel better. Now she is sitting down with them, folks are pampering her and ministering to her, and everything is all right.

I am saying that fear, frustration and aggravated emotional upsets are capable of bringing about accidents, sickness, and disease.

It's not what you eat that causes sickness, it's what eats you emotionally that causes illness.

According to medical science, anger in all degrees, depression and anxiety trigger more fatal heart attacks and place more stress on the heart than any other stimulus including physical exertion and fatigue.[1]

Emotional upsets produce widespread changes in the physical body.

1. It changes blood flowing to an organ of your body.
2. It affects the secretion of certain glands in your body.
3. It changes the tension of muscles in your body.

I have observed these changes and many others in my own life during an emotional upset. Emotional upset produces color change in your body. Whenever I was embarrassed,

---

[1]*Scope*, November 13, 1947

for example, I could feel my blood vessels carrying more blood to my neck, face, and head, which produces blushing.

Emotional upsets often pick adrenal glands as a target. Abnormal secretion of adrenalin can cause high blood pressure, hardening of the arteries, arthritis, ulcers and many other diseases. Emotional upsets can produce tightened muscles. Before I became a Christian I experienced my muscles tightening to the point of producing pain and severe headaches when I became frightened or very angry.

After I became a Christian I realized that I was dealing with something far beyond the reach of medicine. I was dealing with spiritual beings, and in order for me to deal with these powers and principalities, I must have spiritual weapons which Jesus Christ our Lord has provided for us in 2 Corinthians 10:3-5. As I confessed and asked my heavenly Father to forgive me as I forgave myself and all those who had done me wrong, immediately and miraculously God delivered me from all of my emotional upsets, drugs, bleeding ulcer, and paralysis. He replaced it with His love which is the divine medicine for all diseases that the devil puts on us.

Almost two thousand years ago Jesus Christ gave us an answer to our never-failing protection for ourselves from the attacks of the enemy when He said: "Love your God and your neighbor as yourself." Mark 12:30-31 says, **And thou shalt love the Lord thy God with all thy heart...Thou shalt love thy neighbour as thyself....**

The apostle Paul confirms this by saying:

> **Charity** (love) **suffereth long, and is kind; charity envieth not; charity vaunteth not itself, is not puffed up;**
>
> **Doth not behave itself unseemly, seeketh not her own, is not easily provoked, thinketh no evil;**
>
> **Charity never faileth....**
>
> **1 Corinthians 13:4,5,8**

Obedience to the Lord is loving oneself and others, for it will save you from a host of sickeness and diseases. It is the only hope and answer for the people in a sin-sick world.

6
Effects of Fear

Many animals and creeping things use fear to capture their prey. They paralyze them with *fear*. The lion — king of the jungle — can be imprisoned in a flimsy wooden cage. You couldn't hold a lion in a wooden cage. All he has to do to free himself is to smash the wooden bars that imprison him with his giant paw. But the lion doesn't know that. So he remains imprisoned through ignorance and fear.

Don't you see how you and I can be imprisoned in our cages of fear, by nervousness, frustration, bitterness, wrath, anger, clamor, evil speaking, and anxiety? All of these things the devil wants to place upon us, and God is saying: "I want you to be free." All you have to do is start rebelling against the devil and his symptoms and hate them enough to shout, "I have had enough of this, and in the name of Jesus I command you, devil, to take your hands off God's property!" Then start doing the thing you have so long feared to do. You will find that fear has lost its grip!

People go through their lives unfulfilled — half paralyzed because of deep-rooted fears that bring about chemical (reaction) changes.

Let me give you an illustration of how fear can produce sickness and disease. When I worked as a police officer, on several occasions as an investigating officer, I had to inform relatives that their loved one was killed as a result of a car accident, in a gang fight, or while crossing the street. As I was telling them the story, I watched their facial and emotional expression change before my eyes. Some would turn white as a sheet, others would scream and some would faint from the shock.

I recall on one occasion as I walked into the home of a woman who was recovering from the loss of her husband to tell her that her 15-year-old boy had stolen a car and while running away from the police, hit the bridge head on and killed himself. The two individuals that meant everything to her had been snatched away from her in a period of one month. She was completely and irreconcilably overwhelmed with grief and emotional upset, and she refused to listen to anything that I was trying to say. She had to be subdued physically to keep her from taking her own life.

Here we can see that not only emotions of hate, anger, jealousy, unforgiveness, bad tempers are capable of producing serious and fatal diseases, but the emotion of sorrow can also destroy the body by producing abnormal increases of hormones and toxins from adrenal and thyroid glands.

Now suppose you were to receive a visitor that would tell you, "I am sorry to inform you, but your loved one was just killed in a car accident." What would happen to you? Fear would rush in. Perhaps your hair would stand on end, your breathing would become irregular, your heart would start to pound, or your body would feel numb. Some would pass out, and others would develop all kinds of symptoms that would need medical treatment.

Then imagine that half an hour later a message arrives and says, "We are terribly sorry, but we have made a mistake. It was another family that had the same name as yours."

Now what would happen? A great heavy sigh of relief would follow, and your breathing would become normal. Your heart beat would return to normal in a few moments of time, and you would be your old laughing self again, though a little more thankful to God than usual!

What am I trying to show?

I am trying to show that emotional disorders can and do produce sickness and disease in the body. That is why you need the blood of Jesus Christ to wash away your sins.

When His blood washes away your sins, the problem of sin is dealt with. The complex of guilt is gone and you come to peace with God.

Peace I leave with you, my peace I give unto you: not as the world giveth, give I unto you....
John 14:27

Peace with God is as real as you are. It is an experience. And when fear has lost its power over you, you are on your way to being healthy and strong.

Recently, my sister-in-law, Jan, was visiting us with her three small but very beautiful children. In the night as she would put her children to bed, one would cry about, or claim an earache, because the mother had put that child to bed in the dark. The lights were out. Did she really have an earache? Well, she said she did. Something had to be done for her. Either the light had to be turned on or Mama had to go and get in bed with her. When either of these were done, the earache went away and the little child fell off to sleep.

How many times have we given our children an aspirin or some other sedative to get rid of pain that was produced by *fear*? What about the little fellow who has nausea or a terrible stomach pain just before the school bus goes in the morning? Mama hardly knows what to do, for she is upset and is so concerned. She might even call the doctor, but strangely enough, five minutes after the school bus is out of sight, the pain is gone and Johnny is all right.

What you need to do is to face up to the fact that this very selfsame situation carries on into adult life. How often do we avoid our responsibilities as wives, husbands, mothers, fathers and citizens because of our convenient headaches? It if wasn't for that headache, you would have to face a lot of responsibility. (But when things get too much, ''Well, let's have a migraine headache''). A person who is running away from responsibility is driven by the spirit of fear which is of the devil. If you want to be healed and remain whole and enjoy a successful, happy and full life until Jesus comes, you have to get *victory over fear.* You can do this by humbling yourself under the mighty hand of God and casting all your cares on him; for he cares for you! (1 Peter 5:5-7).

Doctors know that many childhood diseases are a product of fear, and if they are not diagnosed as such, they become major illnesses in adult life, both emotionally and physically. Doctors realize this. You go to the doctor with the symptom of high blood pressure, and he asks you, ''What troubles do you have?'' You have ulcers and he asks you, ''What pressures are you under?'' The doctors have learned that not only germs, but emotional disturbances can and do bring about diseases which cannot be cured until negative forces in the mind are removed. No wonder Jesus said, ''Let not your heart be troubled.'' You must stand on the Word of God and boldly declare:

I will not be subjected to this fear.

I will not be a slave to the devil.

I will not accept this suggestion.

And by faith in Christ Triumphant, I have the victory over fear, sicknesses and death itself, for I am a master of all situations *in Jesus name.*

7
Acquired or Hereditary Fear

Consider that a baby is born with just two basic primary fears. We could probably add a few more if we wanted to be scientific, but for our purposes there are two obvious, detectable basic fears. The first fear is that of falling, and the second fear is that of hearing a loud noise. Also, think about all the other fears you may see in a child and sense in yourself.

There are certain fears, of course, that are reasonable (protective fear). If a child has been burned by hot coals, he becomes protectively fearful against touching burning coals again. That's all right, but at times fears become abnormal. When they do, often an evil spirit has taken hold, and that fearful spirit needs to be dealt with.

A famous statesman once said: "We have nothing to fear but fear itself." Satan takes advantage of the fears you permit to come into your life, by bringing with the fear sickness, disease and accidents.

Fear, like faith, has great power, only its influence is negative, working in reverse. Faith is a positive spiritual substance; it is the evidence of things not seen. In contrast, when you are troubled with deep-rooted fears, those fears have the same force and power of attraction as faith — except in reverse. Therefore, fear is the opposite of faith.

Fear is welcomed by many persons as an attractive crutch to draw sympathetic attention to self, and it works like a magnet. That is why the Bible says in Matthew 24:28:

> **For wheresoever the carcase is, there will the eagles be gathered together.**

We never see eagles gather together over a healthy animal, but as soon as the animal gets sick, the buzzards are gathering overhead to attack the animal and to destroy its body, sometimes even before it dies. If this is true in the natural, it's just as true in the spiritual realm. As long as we confess what the Word of God says, the devil and his buzzards cannot attack us. As soon as we confess negatively, we attract the devil, even as the sick animal attracts the buzzards, and he has the legal right to come and attack us with sickness, disease, and even death.

If you fear cancer, you are actually drawing it to you. If you fear a heart attack, you are drawing it to you. If you fear you're going to lose your job, you are drawing the loss of your job toward you. Fear will tear down, whereas faith will build up. Fear will bring about poverty, whereas faith will bring about wealth. Fear will create sickness, whereas faith will create health. Fear will bring about accidents, whereas faith will drive them away.

8
Victory Over Fear

In the book of Job we read that Job confessed fear about his family when he said, **The thing which I greatly feared is come upon me** (Job 3:25). Imagine that. Job says the things he feared finally caught up with him. Keep in mind that we think in terms of pictures. Before you can describe anything, you must first *see* it. Describe a beach, water, sand, or sky that you have seen. The person listening to you takes your words and converts them into his own thought pictures. That is the whole process.

If you say, "I'm sick," then you have seen yourself sick. If you say by faith, "I'm well," you have already seen yourself well by faith (2 Cor. 5:7). Can you tell me why blind people normally don't have wrinkles? It is because they cannot see themselves in a mirror. Every morning as you look into the mirror you say, "My goodness, I am really getting old and gray, aren't I?" You are what you confess with your mouth. The thought gives place to the devil and you thereby give him an opportunity and he will make your hair prematurely gray. If he can make you afraid, he can overcome you. He can paralyze you with fear. He can rob you of a ministry, or joy, or dignity, and he may put your manhood to death.

Now let me give you the cure for fear which is: **the blood of the Lamb and...the word of their testimony...** (Rev. 12:11). The cure for fear is the Word of God. Jesus said in Hebrews 13:5, **I will never leave you nor forsake you.**

Colossians 3:16 says,

> **Let the word of Christ dwell in you richly in all wisdom; teaching and admonishing one another in psalms and hymns and spiritual songs, singing with grace in your heart to the Lord.**

This is the secret. If you want to be free from fear, let the *Word of God* dwell in you richly.

Psalm 23:1 tells us, **The Lord is my shepherd; I shall not want.** The Lord says: **I am the Lord that healeth thee** (Ex. 15:26). The Bible says: **. . . neither shall any plague come nigh thy dwelling** (Ps. 91:10).

Philippians 4:6 says:

> **Be careful for nothing, but in every thing by prayer and supplication and thanksgiving let your requests be made known unto God.**

This means that we have to dwell richly in the Word of God — the Bible.

When Jesus was tempted in the wilderness, He met and defeated the author of fear, Satan, with the Word of God. He said: *It is written,* and then quoted what was written in relation to whatever temptation was presented. Note that Jesus addressed Satan personally, just as we are to do. Satan says, "You will never make ends meet." The Bible says,

> **I have been young, and now am old; yet have I not seen the righteous forsaken, nor his seed begging bread.**
>
> **Psalm 37:25**

Jesus said, **I will never leave thee, nor forsake thee** (Heb. 13:5).

You have to change the thought picture. Fear says, "Well, suppose the money does not come in?" Then you have a picure of money not coming in. In Haggai 2:8, God said, **The silver is mine, and gold is mine.** If you fear that the money won't come in, it won't come in; the devil will see to it, and you can be sure of that. But God said to have a faith image (Rom. 4:17). Job said, "I saw myself losing my children, my cattle, my wife. I saw myself outside the workings of God. The very thing I permitted myself to see came upon me."

Why don't you get rid of that fear image and start seeing God meet all your needs according to his riches in glory? Instead of being fired, why don't you see yourself promoted to a better job?

Instead of seeing your overtime cut, why don't you see yourself getting a pay raise? When you begin to fear, you begin to suppose something — usually bad. Why don't you say, "Suppose the money does come in." Why don't you say, "Suppose God has healed me by faith now." Why don't you say, "Suppose my children are saved by faith now." Instead of being negative, be positive in God.

Someone says: "Suppose I have a heart attack."
"Suppose you don't!"

"Suppose I get fired."
"Suppose you don't!"

Come on; let your supposing be in God!

Ephesians 5:19 says,

> **Speaking to yourselves in psalms and hymns and spiritual songs, singing and making melody in your heart to the Lord.**

Here is another step in your cure for fear — making melody in your heart to the Lord.

> **There is no fear in love; but perfect love casteth out fear: because fear hath torment. He that feareth is not made perfect in love.**
>
> **1 John 4:18**

In Hebrews 13:5 Jesus is quoted, **I will never leave thee, nor forsake thee,** so that we may bodly say, "The Lord is my helper and He is on my side, and I will not fear what men shall do unto me" (Ps. 118:6). God's Word tells us that we are being delivered out of the hand of our enemies, and we are to serve Him without fear (Luke 1:74).

We as Christians must realize that we do not, must not, and should not be moved by what we see or feel, but we should be moved only by what the Word of God tells us. The Word says that we must walk by *faith* and not by sight, for without faith we cannot please God. We should do everything within our power to please God, and not the devil.

We should not confess the lies of the devil, but the Word of God which is in our mouth, and is capable of producing life. **Greater is he that is in you, than he that is in the world** (1 John 4:4).

9
Living Above Fear

Now that you have *victory over fear,* it is imperative that you stand your ground and "fight the good fight of faith."

Remember: All that you are — or ever will be as a Christian — is basically stated in Romans 10:9, ***Confess* with thy mouth. . .*believe* in thine heart.**

The Bible says that **God hath dealt to every man** (to every Christian) ***the measure of faith*** (Rom. 12:3). This means that *you (already) have faith.* You have heard the Gospel; you *"believe in your heart."* Now to make your belief work and bring forth fruit, you must *"confess with your mouth."*

This doesn't mean that you're to confess negativism and fear or failure and defeat — nor does it mean that you're to confess some creed or doctrine (even though these may be good). You must *"confess with thy mouth the Lord Jesus."*

Whatever blessing you claim from God, you must see that Christ purchased this blessing at the cross. In other words, don't seek for an experience, *confess* the Person — *"the Lord Jesus" of Romans 10:9.* When you want forgiveness from sin, don't base your believing on the doctrine of salvation, *look to Christ as your Saviour.* In sickness, *see Him as your Healer.* The same is true with every need you have; you must have a positive confession of faith in Christ's finished work.

Recently, I read a tract by Joe and Dan Ninowshi. It was such a source of inspiration to me that I asked permission to include it in this chapter. Let these truths be *your confession,* too. Read them again and again. Speak them to your friends. This is what God says in His Word. *Act* as though you believe it, and He stands behind it to make it good:

MY CONFESSION OF FAITH according to Philemon 1:6, ''That the communication of my faith may become effectual by my acknowledging every good thing which is in me in Christ Jesus.''

I am now releasing my faith by confessing this to be the greatest day of my life. ''This is the day that the Lord hath made; I will rejoice and be glad in it.''

I am a recreated being, ''old things have passed away and all things have become new.''

I am created into His glorious image and likeness. I am His workmanship and am complete in Christ.

I am full of His Spirit and divine power. I have the fruit of His Spirit, which is love, joy, peace, patience, goodness, kindness, meekness, temperance and faith.

I am humbly submitting myself to the authority of His Holy Word, for He and His Word are one. I am obedient to His commandments, and He enlarges my capacity to receive ''Revelation'' knowledge, wisdom, understanding and ability in all things that pertain to life and Godliness.

I am God's property, I have ''been bought with the blood of the Lord Jesus Christ.'' Therefore, I am free from the curse of the law. Sin, sickness, poverty, fear, doubt, worry, confusion and all that satan represents shall not have dominion over me.

I am prospering in my spirit, soul, body and finances, for I am a liberated person. Jesus said for me to ''know the truth'' and the truth would ''make me free.'' I am ''standing fast in the liberty wherein Christ has made me free.''

I am a disciplined person, I study God's Word daily, I meditate upon its precepts, I confess who Christ is, what He has done and what He is doing in and through me now. I am acting upon truths and I am expecting God to meet all my needs and "to do super-abundantly above all I dare ask, hope, dream or desire" in every area of my life.

I am a beautiful person full of God's forgiveness and love. I forgive as God has forgiven me. I love as God has loved me — therefore, His faith is working in me by love. I speak directly to every mountain of satanic adversity in my life and command them to go in the Name of Jesus. They cannot stay, they must go in Jesus' Name.

Through the abundance of God's grace, I have received the gift of righteousness and am now reigning in this life by Christ Jesus.

In Genesis 1:24-31 and Genesis 2:8-15, God has told me what it was that a righteous man was to reign over. Praise God, I am a righteous person and I am reigning over God's creation now. "Christ has been made worthy to receive power, riches, wisdom, strength, honor, glory and blessing."

I am now a joint heir with Christ and as He is, so am I, in this world. He has made me worthy to receive all that Jesus represents. Praise God, I am everything that the Word delcares that I am. I have communicated my faith by acknowledging every good thing which is in me in Christ Jesus. I believe my faith is now working effectually and that all of my needs and desires have already been supplied by His riches in glory through Christ Jesus. I worship with all my heart, soul and strength. I lift up my voice and hands in praise and adoration to His glorious name for He is worthy of praise and He has made me worthy to praise His name!

So let us seize and hold fast and retain without wavering the hope we cherish and confess, and our acknowledgment of it, for He Who promised us is reliable (sure) and faithful to His word.

Hebrews 10:23 AMP

To contact the author,
write:
Bill Basansky
Love and Grace Fellowship
P. O. Box 7126
Fort Myers, Florida 33911

Please include your prayer requests and comments when you write.

Additional copies are available at your local bookstore or by writing:

Harrison House
P. O. Box 35035 • Tulsa, OK 74153

In Canada, contact:

Word Alive
P. O. Box 284
Niverville, Manitoba
CANADA ROA 1EO

For international sales in Europe, contact:

Harrison House Europe
Belruptstrasse 42 A
A — 6900 Bregenz
AUSTRIA